DON'T WEE
IN THE BATH,
TERRY!

Potty Poems
with a Capital
'P'

by

Gez Walsh

Illustrated by the author

The King's England Press
2003

ISBN 1 872438 99 7

is typeset by Moose Manuscripts
in Times New Roman 14pt and published by
The King's England Press,
Cambertown House, Commercial Road, Goldthorpe,
Rotherham, South Yorkshire, S63 9BL

Printed and bound in Great Britain by:

Woolnough Bookbinding
Irthlingborough
Northamptonshire

Foreword

Please buy this book! I'm being held prisoner in a small dank cell by my publishing company: I have no light, only a candle strapped to my head, and no company except for the rats that come to nibble my toes each night. My publishers say that unless sales of this book are good, I will not be let out to play.

So get out that £4.50 and rush to the counter to buy this book and save a poor man from his terrible fate.

My publishers would like to point out that none of the above is true, and that they are kind, caring people and would never hurt any living thing.

Now will you take these thumb screws off and leave me my bread and water?

Dedication

In memory of my grandma,
Adeline Walsh

Don't Wee in the Bath, Terry!

Don't wee in the bath, Terry,
There's a good fellow;
It makes you smell quite funny
And turns the water yellow.

Don't wee in the bath, Terry,
Whatever you do:
You might end up swallowing it,
So get out and use the loo!

Athletic Feet

Argh! Dad has fungus growing
In between his hairy toes.
Just what sort of health risk
To our family does this man pose?

He says that it's athlete's foot
But him, an athlete?
It takes him all his energy
To get out of his seat!

Dangerous Science

Our science teacher once bet us a pound
That we'd be amazed at a gas he'd found.
But his actions were quite dire
When he tried to set it on fire
And burned our school to the ground.

Danny's Amazing Talking Cabbage

Danny's amazing talking cabbage
Has to be the weirdest thing anyone's seen
As it talks of life in the cabbage patch
And its love affair with a runner bean.

Danny's teachers were first surprised
Then amazed to hear
That the cabbage could do algebra
While quoting the works of Shakespeare.

It said it could tell the future,
But this was not true
Because Danny's mum chopped it up
And made it into a stew!

There's a Mouse in the House!

My Mum is going crazy
Just because she saw a mouse;
We don't know where it is
But it's living in our house.

It is very, very quiet -
Not a sound does it utter,
But it's eating all our food
And poohing in our butter.

Dad wanted to set a trap
Until I said, "You can't do that!"
But the problem was soon solved
When the mouse met our pet cat.

Batty!

"Don't be scared of bats,"
My Dad would always say.
"They're gentle little creatures
And are easily scared away."

But I think he must be crazy
If he expects me to believe that -
I had six stitches in my head
When I was hit by a cricket bat!

Man from Melrose

There was once a man from Melrose,
Who had never ever blown his nose!
He would cough and wheeze,
Once let off a big sneeze
And his snot blew off all of his toes.

Who Nicked Grandad's Gnashers?

Grandad takes out his false teeth
Each and every night,
Then he pops them in a jar
Before he turns out the light.

But when he woke one morning
He knew that something was wrong,
Because when he looked in the jar
He saw that his false teeth had gone!

Just who was the culprit?
Who was that thief
Who had sneaked in in the night
And stolen Grandad's teeth?

I was the first suspect,
I once had an accident, you see.
I once got his teeth stuck up the Hoover,
But this time it wasn't me.

I thought it might be the tooth fairy,
But that would be too drastic.
What self-respecting tooth fairy
Would take teeth made from plastic?

So then we blamed the dog,
But that was beyond belief.
Just what would that crazy mutt
Want with a pair of plastic teeth?

Then in walked my Grandma
Saying her dentures were giving her grief.
They were loose and rubbing her gums -URGH!
She was wearing Grandad's teeth!

My Old Man's Van

My old man
Had a rusty old van
That rattled and shook
Like an old tin can.
Its doors didn't fit
Just quite right,
It had one screen wiper
And one headlight.
It billowed out smoke
That made him cough
And sounded like a tank
Since the exhaust fell off,
With tyres so bald
It was hard to steer,
The brakes didn't work,
It was missing one gear.
He would soon get rid
Is what dad had planned,
But the police stopped him:
Now from driving he's banned!

I'm Bored

I'm so bored
I could sleep forever.
I'm so bored
I could discuss the weather.
I'm so bored
I could count to a million.
I'm so bored
I could paint the park pavilion.
I'm so bored
Because I'm so cool,
I'm always this bored
When I'm at school.

Just the Three of Us

I live in a nice house,
There's my Mum, my Sis and me.
That's the way I like it,
It's good with just us three.

My Mum is just brilliant
Saying, "It's better being man-free."
But I don't know what she's on about -
The man of the house is me!

The Snog

Snog, snog, snog, snog
Is all my brother and his girlfriend do.
Snog, snog, snog, snog -
I think their mouths are stuck together with glue.

Has Bean?

I don't know if broad beans are broad
Or whether runner beans run,
But I know that if you eat baked beans
They give you an exploding bum!

She Loves Me, She Loves Me Not

To find if your girlfriend loves you
This is what you should do:
Buy her a big box of chocolates
And see if she shares them with you.

If she takes them home
And shares them with her mother,
Dump her straight away
And then find yourself another.

Steve and his Secret Agent Underpants

Steve was an odd sort of boy
But not without his charms,
Though his Mum wished he didn't have underpants
That finished just beneath his arms.

But Steve would not remove them;
When asked he would just make excuses,
Because Steve was a secret agent
And his underpants had many uses.

He was once on a mission,
On orders the Prime Minister had sent.
For shelter he whipped off his underpants
Then made them into a tent.

When he needed food,
To fill his empty dish,
He threw his underpants in a lake
And trawled up lots of fish.

Then the enemy nearly caught him
On this mission he must not fail,
But he escaped in a little boat
Using his underpants as a sail.

He later fell in love with an agent,
She was Russian and oh, so cute!
She later tried to kill him on an airplane
But he escaped with his underpants parachute.

So if you see a young boy
With his underpants up his chest,
Just keep well away from him
If you know what's for the best.

Bad Habits

There was once a little dragon
That caused his Mum to dread.
She was always telling him off
For smoking at night in bed.

"We only breathe out fire
To scare the people of the town.
You don't do it at home
Unless you want to burn it down!"

"So no more smoking in bed,
Please give me your assurance.
Because if you burn this cave down
We're not covered by the insurance."

The Ballad of Annie and Arnie

In an old folks home,
Sat in front of a TV,
Was old Annie Wright
Aged one-hundred-and-three.
She was watching a soap,
Thinking it so boring,
Surrounded by old folk,
Most of them snoring,

When into the room
Walked old Arnold Pine.

He was a good-looking man
And glad to be alive,
Had an eye for the ladies:
He was one-hundred-and-five.
Weighing eight stones
He was tall and thin,
Set eyes on old Annie
Before he moved in.

This man couldn't afford
To waste any time.

Annie threw him a smile
As Arnie danced a jig;
She thought he looked cool
In his Elvis wig.
Annie clutched her heart
Saying, "It's beyond belief.
A man's chatting me up,
And he has all his own teeth!"

Then they held hands
And kissed.

They just fell in love
But they didn't have long;
They wanted to get wed,
People thought it wrong
That two old folk
Well past their prime
Should be kissing and cuddling
Nearly all the time.

At their time of life
They should be knitting.

The matron of the home
Thought it was appalling
So she picked up the phone
And then she started calling.
She called Annie's boys,
They were Reg and Ron:
Reg was seventy-nine,
Ron was eighty-one.

These boys were trouble
With a capital 'T'.

The boys walked in
To spoil Annie's fun
Saying, "Who's this man
That's snogging our mum?"
Arnie put up his fists
Saying, "You'd better flee,
I was a world champion boxer
Back in twenty-three."

But the boys thought
That they could take him.

The matron stepped in
Saying, "You've nothing to prove.
Arnie, pack up your things,
You'll have to move.
You're not welcome here
When you behave like that."
Then she winked at the boys -
What a dirty little rat!

Annie rose to her feet
Then the lady cried:

"How could you be so cruel
To your old mum?
Deny me any love
And deny me fun."
Arnie was shown the door;
He gave Ron a smack.
Then he shouted out to Annie,
"My love, I'll be back!"

Our hero was always
True to his word.

Arnie came back that night
Armed with a gift;
He sneaked upstairs
On a Stannah stair lift.
He walked on the landing
By the light of the moon,
Pulled out a wedding ring
Then entered Annie's room.

He asked her to marry him;
She said 'yes', of course.

So they eloped that night,
Off to Gretna Green,
And got themselves hitched -
It was like a dream.
They spent their last days
Full of love and glory,
But there is a moral
To this little story:

Live out your dreams
Even when you are young,
And make sure your kids
Are not like Reg and Ron.

Life's Great Mysteries

Why do boys think that farting is funny?
Why does bottled water cost so much money?
Why do girls paint their faces?
Why do men in flash cars wear red braces?
Who wears jeans with an elastic waist?
Who thinks broccoli is a nice taste?
Why do women wear shoes that could cripple?
And why on earth does a man need a nipple?

Mad Dog Mum

Don't be cruel to animals
Was a belief of my Mum,
But when our dog weed on the carpet
She kicked it up the bum!

I Love Bullies

Bullies are cool,
Bullies are ace,
Bullies like to punch you
In the face.

They take your money
And rough you up
If you dare tell a teacher
And grass them up.

I love bullies,
They're so full of charm.
Now that I've written this
Will you stop breaking my arm?

The Bogeyman

"The bogeyman will get you!"
My mother always said.
"The bogeyman will get you
From underneath your bed."

"The bogeyman will get you
Without so much as a peep."
And my mother can't understand
Why I find it so hard to sleep!

Two Pets in One

I said a prayer for my goldfish
Because last night it died;
We buried it in the garden,
I just cried and cried.

Now I don't like our cat,
In fact I really hate it
Because it dug up my goldfish
Then went and ate it!

I Love Lisa

I love Lisa Morgan,
She's so gentle and kind;
But she doesn't like me,
She thinks I'm a pain in the behind!

Big Bad Avril

Avril is such a thug
Who makes a lot of noise,
She scares all the girls away
Then beats up all the boys.

People run and hide
When she walks out of the door;
She walks like a gorilla
Dragging her knuckles on the floor.

She's the world's worst bully,
Her grunting is consistent.
Even teachers are scared of big Avril
The world's worst playground assistant!

The World's Worth Crime

All over the world
It was on everyone's lips:
Just who was it
That had nicked the Queen's chips?

Was it her butler
With his shifty eyes?
Was it the chambermaid
Who had nicked those fries?

The police were called
To sort out this crime;
The culprit was caught,
Now he's doing time.

It was her number one corgi
Who'd nicked for no reason.
The queen thought it disgusting -
This amounted to treason!

He's now locked in the tower,
On a cold floor he kips.
No one messes with the Queen
And nicks her chips!

Being a Girl

"Your skirt's too short!"
Complains my Dad.
"You wear too much make-up!"
He drives me mad.

The man's insane,
He's the brain of a pea.
Mum said, "I was like her,
And you fancied me."

Dad said, "That was different!"
Then got all in a whirl
When I told him he knew nothing
About being a young girl!

Gnome Sweet Gnome

Gerald was a strange gnome,
He was no one's son.
Gerald was so different
Because he was six-foot-one.

He sat on his mushroom
His eyes full of tears,
Holding out his fishing rod
With his knees behind his ears.

No one would employ him
To sit in their garden for hours
Because he blocked out the sunlight
And trampled on the flowers.

So he just wanders lonely
With his bright red pointy hat,
Carrying his fishing rod
While being followed by his cat.

He wants gnomes to accept him
So he's starting up a movement;
He wants them all to take a course
In a little gnome improvement.

It Wasn't Me!

It wasn't me!
I wasn't there.
I never did it,
Honest, I swear!
I'm not to blame,
I cross my heart,
It was someone else
Who did that fart!

Fallen Angel

I thought that heaven must be missing an angel
When I saw you walk in here tonight,
But heaven must be missing its only angel
That just loves to start a fight!

Matching Socks

I couldn't find any clean socks
This morning when I got out of bed,
So on my left foot I wore a blue sock
And on my right I wore one red.

At school I met my brother
Who said, "I had the same problem as you,
Only on my left foot I have a red sock
And on my right one a blue."

There's No One Quite Like Grandad

Grandad has a great big nose,
He looks like a sundial in the sun.
He often hangs coats on it
Which he does just for fun.

Grandad has a big bald head
That is so shiny and bright.
Grandma reads her books by it,
It's better than any light.

Grandad has no teeth at all,
Not one tooth in his head,
But he couldn't care less:
"The tooth fairy made me rich," he said.

Grandad has a great big belly,
The biggest belly you've ever seen.
I used to jump up and down on it,
It was the world's best trampoline.

Grandad is the best person in the world
But grandma must be a bit dim;
She must have known some ugly blokes
For her to ever fancy him!

The One that Got Away

I once caught a fish
With a rod and reel;
I sat there for ages
Waiting to make a steal,
But my Mum got angry
And gave me a smack
Then told me to go to the bowl
And put the goldfish back.

The Evil Poet

People say that my poems are rude
And that all my rhymes are far too crude.
Why do these people take such a huff
When me, myself, couldn't give a stuff?

The Cat Bath

I shampooed my cat -
He gave me a look so stuffy.
So I gave him a blow dry
And now I call him Fluffy.

Never Trust...

Never trust a crocodile that wears sunglasses,
You cannot tell what he's thinking;
He'll sneak up while you're swimming,
Then he'll sink his teeth in.

Never trust a bumble bee with a baseball bat,
It's not used for making honey;
He will fly out of a daffodil
And with his bat demand all your money.

Never trust a worm with a hand grenade,
He won't say please or pardon,
But late at night he comes out to fight
And blows massive holes in your garden.

Never ever trust a teacher on a Friday,
After a hard week you deserve a rest;
Then your teacher says, with a great big grin,
"Now, class, it's time to take a test."

The Origin of Babies

Dad says babies are found in the cabbage patch
And that they feed on cabbage hearts;
That would explain why my baby sister
Lets off such humungous farts.

Mum says the stork brings you babies.
This, I think, could be true,
Because my sister often flaps her arms
When she has a pooh.

My cousin says babies live in your mum's belly.
Good grief is that boy sick!
How would a baby get into a belly?
He must think that I'm really thick.

A Cleaner Rose

There was once a cleaner called Rose
Who would Hoover the floor with her nose.
People thought her amazing,
It's just like she's grazing
While wiping the walls with her toes.

Salad

Mum says, "Eat more salad."
I think that she's gone mad.
She reckons that if I just eat burgers
I'll end up fat like my dad.

But I hate eating salad,
It makes me feel so glum,
And no one else eats salad
Except my rabbit and my Mum.

Uncle Stephen

I love my Uncle Stephen,
I think that he's so cool
But my Dad doesn't like him,
He says that he's a fool.

Dad says that it's not normal
For a man to be like him,
But Stephen is kind and funny
While my Dad is rather dim.

Stephen lives in a big house
Having the best that money can buy,
He shares it with his best friend,
A hairdresser named Guy.

When they come to visit us
Dad says they look a sight,
With a piercing through their eyebrow
And jeans that are far too tight.

But Stephen isn't bothered,
He says there's lots of people like dad
Who can't accept people for what they are
And live their lives so sad.

Belt Up

While we were on holiday
My dad, the stupid fool,
Bought a snake-skin belt -
He thought that it looked cool.

He asked me what I thought;
It was more than I could take.
I told him that I thought snake-skin
Looked far better on the snake.

Henry Meeks

On a faraway mountain
Lived a young lad
Who had a strange problem
Which made him so sad.

People would avoid him,
Poor little Henry Meeks,
Because when he walked
His bum made little squeaks.

He had seen many doctors
From England to France,
But none could cure him
Of the squeak in his pants.

He'd been given many lotions
To stop those bum squeaks:
None of them worked
But he had very soft bum cheeks.

All the people of his village
Thought him a freak
When he shouted, "Hello!"
Followed by a little bum squeak.

But Henry was a brave boy,
As the villagers would soon find.
He wasn't stupid and useless
But courageous and kind.

One day a terrible blizzard
Raged high on the mountain
As the local search team
Gathered by the village fountain.

They were to look for an actor
Who thought he was so cool,
But you should never climb alone,
Not unless you're a fool.

So they set off to search
And find this stupid man
But Henry was ahead of them,
He was the actor's biggest fan.

Henry knew the mountain well
And climbed like a mountain goat
With blankets and hot drinks
Wrapped up in his wool coat.

As Brave Henry moved on
Climbing higher and higher
The blizzard it howled,
His situation became dire.

Then Henry saw a movement
From inside a small cave -
The actor had been found
By a small boy so brave.

The actor was injured,
He gave a small yelp.
His voice had been lost
Through calling for help.

Henry wrapped him in blankets
And gave him a hot drink
Then thought, "What do I do?
Come on, think, Henry, think!"

Then Henry saw the lights
Of the search party team;
He tried to attract them
With scream after scream

But the blizzard was fierce,
His screaming was drowned;
He knew to attract their attention
He needed a high pitched sound.

It was then that he saw it
In that cave so glum:
He'd found a large goat horn
Which he put to his bum.

The actor couldn't believe it!
He thought his future looked bleak
As Henry marched with the horn to his bum
Shouting, "Squeak, bum, Squeak!"

So the search party moved on
As if playing hide and seek
When the leader shouted, "Hush!
What is that loud squeak?"

Then a man started laughing
Saying, "I'm cold and I'm numb,
But don't you recognise that noise?
It's little Henry Meek's bum!"

So through the raging blizzard
They fought without fear,
Following the squeaks
From Henry Meek's rear.

So the actor was saved,
Henry had shown them the way,
But that was many years ago:
What does he do today?

Well, Henry's now a big man,
He's the greatest mountain guide.
Tourists follow him up the mountain
By the squeaks from his backside!

Driving Me Clean Round the U Bend

There's a monster down our toilet,
I know that this is true.
Now I'm scared to have a wee,
I'm scared to have a pooh.

Dad says that I'm being silly,
There's nothing down our loo,
Except for water and wee wee
And the occasional number two.

But I'm not taking any chances,
At night I hear it hum;
I know that it's there waiting
To jump out and bite my bum!

Scary Word

Lots of words are scary,
Like monster, vampire or ghost,
But none of these bother me -
I'll tell you what scares me most.

It's a word I dare not mention,
A word you don't want to hear,
It's when the doctor tells you:
"I'm afraid you have diarrhoea!"

Rita

There was once a Spanish girl, Rita,
Who had a boyfriend called Peter.
To tell you the truth
She had only one tooth
And so Peter called her "One-Eater"!

Dead Skinny

Barney was a skeleton,
Nothing but dry white bones.
He lived in a damp crypt
And would love to flit
But skeletons can't buy homes.

Barney had a skeleton dog,
He would walk it late at night.
All the people would shout,
"There's a skeleton about!"
Then they would faint with fright.

Barney eats lots of fatty foods
Because his thinks he's too thin,
But the more he ate
He became more irate
As the food fell out under his chin.

Barney was a total loner,
"I've never had friends," he said.
From him people would hide
He doesn't know he once died
And no one dare tell him he's dead.

Quackers!

Our doctor must be a duck:
Dad went to him with a bad back,
The doctor said there was nothing wrong.
Dad said that he's a quack?

Mum Dad?

My Dad was going to a fancy dress.
My Mum said, "You're not wearing those!"
He looked just like a gorilla
But he was wearing women's clothes.

My Dad he looked so scary,
He looked so out of place.
Have you ever seen a big hairy man
With lots of make-up on his face?

But what worried Mum the most,
What really made her ill
Was that a sixteen-stone man in a dress
Reminded her of Dad's Auntie Gill!

Sea Weed

I don't want to be a fish
Swimming in the sea.
Who wants to spend their life
Swimming in their own wee?

Fibs Without Ribs

Ghosts can never be liars
No matter what they do;
They always tell you stories
That are easy to see straight through.

Boy Named Paul

There was once a boy named Paul
Who had no manners at all.
He let off a big fart
Which blew his trousers apart
And left a big hole in the wall.

The Crash Diet

Colin was a monster fish
And rather smug and fat,
But he then lost two stones
And is now just skin and bones
Because he was eaten by our cat.

Bad Breff

I've got bad breff,
I've got bad breff.
If I breeve on you
It could cause deff.

I don't know why
It smells so bad;
If I could stop it smelling
I would be so glad.

I brush my teeff,
Use mouffwash too,
But still my mouff
Smells like our loo!

I can't get a girl
To give me a snog
When I've worse breff
Than my stinky dog!

Mum says to change my diet,
Change it in a hurry.
I don't see why -
I only eat garlic and curry!

Cool Fool

There was once a life-guard named Lance
Who loved to swagger and prance.
He thought he looked cool
When he dived into the pool
But we laughed when he lost his pants.

Sweet Maths

Teacher said, "If you had forty cakes
And ate thirty really quick
What would that leave you?"
I said it would leave me feeling sick!

Wash It!

I can wash the sweat from under my armpits,
I can wash the fruit from between my toes,
But, no matter how hard I try,
I can't wash the snot from up my nose.

The Food Chain

The lion had a pooh,
A fly ate the pooh,
A lizard ate the fly,
A snake ate the lizard,
A mongoose ate the snake,
A lion ate the mongoose,
Then the lion had a pooh,
A fly ate the pooh...

High Hopes

We never win at football,
No matter how we try.
I think it's because our goalkeeper
Is only three feet high!

Funny Bunny

Welsh rabbits are so strange
But I like them the most,
Because if you ever cook one
It tastes just like cheese on toast.

Pretty Polly

"Pretty Polly, pretty Polly!"
Is all my parrot will say.
"Pretty Polly, pretty Polly!"
Each and every day.

"Pretty Polly, pretty Polly"
The words ring round my head.
I don't know why he says this
Because we call him Fred!

Big Nose

My Dad has a big nose,
It's shiny and big and round.
It measures half an inch
But that's starting from the ground!

Goodbye, Dad

My Dad hit my Mum one night,
He really made her cry.
Then he ran from the house,
He never said 'goodbye'.

That was quite a while ago,
He never came back home.
I'm now scared and frightened
That Mum and me are all alone.

Mum says she doesn't want him back
And that we have each other at least,
But when Dad's sober he's so gentle
Though when he's drunk he's a beast.

I still hear Mum cry at night
When she thinks that I'm asleep,
All her pain and misery
To herself she tries to keep.

How could he do this to us?
I think the drink is sending him mad.
But for lots of my friends it's the same:
There are lots of men like Dad.